SHORT BLACKS are gems of recent
Australian writing – brisk reads that quicken
the pulse and stimulate the mind.

SHORT BLACKS

CYPHERPUNK REVOLUTIONARY

ON
JULIAN
ASSANGE

ROBERT
MANNE

SHORT ● BLACKS

Published by Black Inc.,
an imprint of Schwartz Publishing Pty Ltd
37–39 Langridge Street
Collingwood VIC 3066 Australia
enquiries@blackincbooks.com
www.blackincbooks.com

First published in the *Monthly*, March 2011.
This edition published 2015.

National Library of Australia Cataloguing-in-Publication entry :
Manne, Robert (Robert Michael), 1947– author.
The cypherpunk revolutionary : on Julian Assange / Robert Manne.
9781863957717 (paperback) 9781925203554 (ebook)
Short blacks ; no.9.
Assange, Julian. WikiLeaks (Organization) Publishers and publishing.
Web publishing. Leaks (Disclosure of information)
070.57973

Cover and text design by Peter Long.

ROBERT MANNE's many books include *Making Trouble* and *The Words That Made Australia* (as co-editor). He is the author of three Quarterly Essays, *In Denial*, *Sending Them Home* and *Bad News*.

Less than twenty years ago Julian Assange was sleeping rough. Even a year ago hardly anyone knew his name. Today he is one of the best-known and most-respected human beings on earth. Assange was the overwhelming winner of the popular vote for *Time* magazine's "Person of the Year" and *Le Monde*'s less politically correct "Man of the Year". If Rupert Murdoch, who recently turned eighty, is the most influential Australian of the post-war era, Julian Assange, who will soon turn forty, is undoubtedly the most consequential Australian of the present time.

Murdoch's importance rests in his responsibility for injecting, through Fox News, the poison of rabid populist conservatism into the political culture of the United States; Assange's in the revolutionary threat that his idea of publishing damaging documentary information sent by anonymous insiders to WikiLeaks poses to governments and corporations across the globe.

Julian Assange has told the story of his childhood and adolescence twice, most recently to a journalist from the *New Yorker*, Raffi Khatchadourian, and some fifteen years ago, secretly but in greater detail, to Suelette Dreyfus, the author of a fascinating book on the first generation of computer hacking, *Underground*, for which Assange was the primary researcher. In what is called the "Researcher's Introduction", Assange begins with a cryptic quote from Oscar Wilde: "Man is least himself when he talks in his own person. Give him a mask, and he will tell you the truth." Nothing about Assange has ever been straightforward. One of the main characters in *Underground* is the Melbourne hacker Mendax. Although there is no way readers at that time could have known it, Mendax is Julian Assange. Putting Khatchadourian and Dreyfus together, and adding a little detail from a blog that Assange published on the internet in 2006–07 and checking it against commonsense and some material that has emerged since his rise to fame, the story of Assange's childhood and adolescence can be told in some detail. There is, however, a problem. Journalists as senior as David Leigh of the *Guardian* or John F. Burns of the *New York Times* in general accept on trust many of Assange's stories about himself. They do not understand that, like many natural writers, he has fashioned his life into a fable.

According to Assange, his mother, Christine Hawkins, left her Queensland home for Sydney at the age of seventeen, around 1970, at the time of the anti–Vietnam War movement when the settled culture of the Western world was breaking up. Christine's father, Dr Warren Hawkins, was the principal of the Northern Rivers College of Advanced Education; her mother was a specialist in medieval literature. Christine fell in love with a man called John Shipton in Sydney. A year or so after Julian was born, in Townsville, they parted. Assange did not meet Shipton again till he was twenty-five.

When Julian was about one, Christine met and married a roving theatrical producer and member of what was by now called the counter-culture, Brett Assange. According to what Julian told Khatchadourian, Brett was the descendant of a Chinese immigrant who had settled on Thursday Island, Ah Sang or Mr Sang. Together Brett and Christine travelled around the country, performing. He painted a vivid portrait for Khatchadourian of an idyllic life after the family settled for a time on Magnetic Island. "Most of this time was pretty Tom Sawyer. I had my own horse. I built my own raft. I went fishing. I was going down mine shafts and tunnels." To Dreyfus, Julian claimed his stepfather was a decent man but also an alcoholic. By the time he was addressing audiences worldwide, his "father" – which Assange informed me is an amalgam of Brett Assange and John Shipton, created to protect their identities – had become idealised as a "good and generous man" who had taught him the most fundamental lesson in life: to nurture victims rather than to create them. Assange also told Dreyfus about a foundational political memory, an incident that had occurred while he was about four but was much spoken of later. His mother and a male friend had discovered evidence concerning the British atomic bomb tests that had taken place in Maralinga in greatest secrecy, which they intended to give to an Adelaide journalist. The male friend had been beaten by police to silence him. Christine had been warned that she was in danger of being charged with being "an unfit mother". She was advised to stay out of politics.

When Julian was eight or nine years old, Christine and Brett Assange separated and then divorced. His mother now formed a "tempestuous" relationship with an amateur musician, Keith Hamilton, with whom she had another child, a boy. To Dreyfus, Julian described Hamilton as a "manipulative and violent psychopath". A brief bitter battle over access to Julian's half-brother was fought. Christine's family was now once more on the move – this time not as before on a "happy-go-lucky odyssey", but hiding on both sides

of the continent in permanent terror. In his
final years of education Julian was home-
schooled or independently educated either
by professors encountered on their travels or
by following his curiosity in public libraries.
He did, however, attend very many schools.
According to Dreyfus, by the time Mendax
was fifteen he "had lived in a dozen different
places" and had "enrolled in at least as many
different schools". His lawyer in his trial
of 1996, Paul Galbally, also told the court
Assange had been enrolled in about twelve
schools. By 2006, Assange claimed he had
attended thirty-seven different schools. To
answer my doubt, Assange explained: "Since
my mother was going to be a witness and
could only reliably remember the schools I
had spent a long time at . . . we claimed merely
twelve to be safe. The figure of 37 includes
schools I spent a single day attending."

One of the schools Julian attended was

in rural Victoria. In the blog he posted on 18 July 2006, there is an account of his and another outsider's experience at this school.

> We were bright sensitive kids who didn't fit into the dominant sub-culture and fiercely castigated those who did as irredeemable boneheads.
>
> This unwillingness to accept the authority of a peer group considered risible was not appreciated. I was quick to anger and brutal statements such as "You're a bunch of mindless apes out of Lord of the Flies" when faced with standover tactics were enough to ensure I got into a series of extreme fights and I wasn't sorry to leave when presented with the dental bills of my tormentors.

Eventually Julian's family settled on the outskirts of Melbourne in Emerald and then

Tecoma, according to Dreyfus. Christine bought Julian a $700 computer and a modem. Assange fell in love with a 16-year-old girl, Teresa, whom he claims to have met through a program for gifted children. He left home and then married his girlfriend. They had a son. This was the period when the underground sub-culture of hacking was forming in Melbourne. Around 1988 Assange joined it under the handle Mendax. By October 1989 an attack was mounted from Australia on the NASA computer system via the introduction of what was called the WANK worm in an attempt to sabotage the Jupiter launch of the Galileo rocket as part of an action of anti-nuclear activists. No one claimed responsibility for this attack, which is outlined in the first chapter of *Underground*. In a Swedish television documentary, *WikiRebels*, made with Assange's co-operation, there are hints he was responsible.

Mendax formed a closed group with two other hackers – Trax and Prime Suspect. They called themselves the International Subversives. According to Dreyfus, their politics were fiercely anti-establishment; their motive adventure and intellectual curiosity; their strict ethic not to profit by their hacking or to harm the computers they entered. Mendax wrote a program called Sycophant. It allowed the International Subversives to conduct "massive attacks on the US military". The list of the computers they could recall finding their way into "read like a Who's Who of the American military-industrial complex". Eventually Mendax penetrated the computer system of the Canadian telecommunications corporation Nortel. It was here that his hacking was first discovered. The Australian Federal Police conducted a long investigation into the International Subversives, Operation Weather. Eventually Trax lost his nerve and began to talk. He told the police that the International Subversives had been hacking on a scale never achieved before. In October 1991 the Australian Federal Police raided Prime Suspect's and Mendax's homes. They found Assange in a state of near mental collapse. His young wife had recently left him, taking their son Daniel. Assange told Dreyfus that he had been dreaming incessantly of "police raids ... of shadows in the pre-dawn darkness, of a gun-toting police squad bursting through his backdoor at 5 a.m." When the police arrived, the incriminating disks, which he had been in the habit of hiding inside a beehive, were scattered by his computer. The evidence was removed.

Assange descended into a personal hell. He was admitted briefly to hospital, suffering from what Suelette Dreyfus describes as "a deep depression and consuming rage". He tried and failed to return home to live with his mother. He frequently slept along Merri Creek in Melbourne or in Sherbrooke Forest. He told Dreyfus that 1992 was "the worst year in his life". The formal charges against Assange were not laid until July 1994. His case was not finally settled until December 1996. Although Assange had been speaking in secretive tones about the technical possibility of a massive prison sentence, in the end he received a $5000 good behaviour bond and a $2100 reparations fine. The experience of arrest and trial nonetheless scarred his soul and helped shape his politics. In his blog of 17 July 2006, Assange wrote:

> If there is a book whose feeling captures me it is First Circle by Solzhenitsyn.
>
> To feel that home is the comraderie [sic] of persecuted, and in fact, prosecuted, polymaths in a Stalinist labor camp! How close the parallels to my

own adventures! ... Such prosecution in youth is a defining peak experience. To know the state for what it really is! To see through that veneer the educated swear to disbelieve in but still slavishly follow with their hearts! ... True belief only begins with a jackboot at the door. True belief forms when lead [sic] into the dock and referred to in the third person. True belief is when a distant voice booms "the prisoner shall now rise" and no one else in the room stands.

No doubt the experience of investigation and prolonged trial was harrowing. Nonetheless, this is a rather self-dramatising passage. Solzhenitsyn was incarcerated in the Gulag Archipelago, harassed for years by the KGB and eventually expelled from the Soviet Union. Assange was investigated by the AFP and received a good behaviour bond and a fine.

*

Julian Assange was extremely sensitive about any public discussion of his impending trial. In 1994 he offered to assist the director of *Dogs in Space*, Richard Lowenstein, with a film about hackers. Assange spoke about the 290 years he might theoretically spend in prison. He learned that Lowenstein had not kept this information confidential. He was furious. He sent Lowenstein a series of threatening emails in which he outlined details of Lowenstein's sexual life. Assange explained to me he did so to make Lowenstein aware of "the significance of his confidentiality breach by way of analogy". Lowenstein protested. Had Assange no understanding of the concept of privacy? Privacy, Assange replied, is "relative". "I could monitor your keystrokes, intercept your phone and bug your residence. If I could be bothered... As one who's has [sic] one's life monitored pretty closely, you quickly come to the realisation that trying to achieve complete privacy is impossible." If Lowenstein wanted to keep details of his life confidential he should use encrypted email. Lowenstein told Assange he had not realised that the information was confidential. "I do not doubt your reasons were not malicious. Stupidity, ignorance and lack of respect come to mind. You seem to think I have only one life. I have many."

While awaiting trial, Julian Assange began to try to reconstruct his life. One overwhelming preoccupation was the bitter struggle waged for the custody of his son, Daniel. In their struggle, Julian and Christine Assange formed a small activist group – Parent Inquiry into Child Protection. They found sources of support inside the Victorian Department of Health and Community Services. An insider provided them with a document of great value to their cause – an internal departmental manual outlining the current rules determining custody disputes. He told Dreyfus that in his fight against government corruption in Victoria he had "acted as a conduit for leaked documents". On several occasions recently, in answering questions about the origin of WikiLeaks, Assange has spoken of a domain site registered in 1999, but with which he did nothing, known as "leaks.org". His interest in leaks must have preceded that. In November 1996 he sent the following enigmatic message to those on certain email lists he had created.

> A few pointy heads in Canberra have been considering your moderator's continued existence. Consequentially I've been called on to justify labour and resources spent on all projects under my control, particularly those that can't easily be quantified such as IQ, BOS, LACC, IS, LEAKS...

All these lists were connected to an internet service provider, Suburbia Public Access
Network, for which Assange was, as he puts
it, "the chief technical brains" and which he
had taken over when its original owner, Mark
Dorset, went to live in Sydney. He likened it to
a "low cost power-to-the-people enabling technology". Suburbia was the vehicle for several
email lists – Interesting Questions (IQ), Best
of Security (BOS), Legal Aspects of Computer Crime (LACC), Inside-Source (IS) and,
presumably, LEAKS – that Assange created.
It was also the free site for several groups of
Melbourne activists, artists and others – the
Powerline Action Group; the Alternative
Technology Association; the Centre for Contemporary Photography; the Australian Public
Access Network Association and, strangely
enough, the Private Inquiry Agents Association. It is because of the continued existence
on the internet of some of the commentary he

wrote for these lists in his mid-twenties that we can begin to hear, for the first time, the distinctive political voice of Julian Assange. In general, it is intelligent and assured. One of Suburbia's clients had published some of the Church of Scientology's holy scriptures. The church threatened legal action against Suburbia. The client, Dave Gerard, fought back. In March 1996, Assange issued an appeal to join an anti-Scientology protest.

> What you have then is a Church based on brainwashing yuppies and other people with more money than sense ... If Nicole Kiddman [sic], Kate Cerbrano [sic], John Travolta, Burce [sic] Willis, Demi Moore and Tom Cruise want to spend their fortunes on learning that the earth is in reality the destroyed prison colony of aliens from outer space then so be it. However, money brings

power and attracts the corrupt . . .
Their worst critic at the moment is
not a person, or an organisation but a
medium – the Internet. The Internet
is by its very nature a censorship free
zone . . . The fight against the Church is
far more than the Net versus a bunch of
wackos. It is about corporate suppres-
sion of the Internet and free speech. It is
about intellectual property and the big
and rich versus the small and smart.

At this time, to judge by the pieces he wrote
that have survived, Assange's main political preoccupation seems to have been the
extraordinary democratic possibilities of
the information-sharing virtual communities across the globe created by the internet,
and the threat to its freedom and flourishing
posed by censorious states, greedy corporations and repressive laws.

Not everything Assange wrote at this time was serious. He was interested in a computer security software program developed by Dan Farmer of Silicon Graphics known as SATAN. One evening in April 1995 he composed "The Dan Farmer Rap" for "firewalls", a list to which he subscribed.

> I'm Dan Farmer you can't fool me —
> The only security consultant to be on MTV,
>
> I've got red hair – hey hands off man!
> don't touch the locks of the mighty Dan.
>
> AC/DC – from the front or from behind,
> you can fuck my arse but you can't touch my mind.
> philosophy's the trip – evil 'n' stuff,
> god, we know a lot, Mike me and Muff.

A real ardent feminist – just like she tells
me to be,
See me out there rooting for sexual
e-qual-ity...

I coded it all – yes the mighty Dan did it
alone,
if you can't believe it, you and your note
pad can fuck off home.

I'm Dan Farmer – now take that down –
it's not every
day you get to interview the world's
biggest security clown.

Several subscribers to "firewalls" were
appalled. One wrote: "Just reading this made
me feel dirty. In 20+ years associated with
this business, I don't think I've ever seen
debate among professionals degraded to
quite this slime-ball level. Mr Assange is an

unprincipled ass . . ." Assange wrote a sort-of apology. "It was perhaps an error of judgment on my behalf to equate the people on this list with those who knew myself and Dan more fully. Such mistakes are ripe to happen when one is merry and full of wine in the wee hours of the morning." Nonetheless, he expressed high amusement regarding all those who had publicly condemned him while privately sending their congratulations. "You know who you are." Assange's Dan Farmer "peccadillo" was still remembered six years later by a British computer geek, Danny O'Brien.

By 1997 Julian Assange, with his friends Suelette Dreyfus and Ralf Weinmann, had written Rubberhose, a piece of "deniable cryptography" for human rights activists and troublemakers, the purpose of which was to make it impossible for torturers or their victims to know whether all the encrypted data on a computer hard drive had been revealed. It was designed to make torture to extract passwords pointless, and defection and betrayal in the face of such torture impossible. The concept was Assange's. Assange argued a convoluted and rather improbable psychological case about why Rubberhose would cause rational torturers to put away their weapons. Danny O'Brien captured the obvious objection rather well. Despite Rubberhose's deniable cryptography, "won't rational torturers just beat you up 'forever'?" Assange disagrees. "Rational torturers have opportunity costs and understand them."

I am in no position to judge the sophistication of the Rubberhose software or the level of creativity it required. I can however assess the quality of the posting announcing its creation, which Assange sent to the firewalls list in June 1997. Assange called it "One Man's Search for a Cryptographic Mythology".

His search to find a suitable name for Rubberhose takes him, in a zany and hilarious stream of consciousness, on a journey through Greek and Roman mythology, the incestuous Cerberus and the clichéd Janus; to the moral pessimism of David Hume, who argued the inescapable connection between joy and despondency; to an unexplained rejection of his request for mythological advice by the Princeton History Department; to Sigmund Freud, the Medusa's Head and the castration complex; to a spoof on Zen Buddhism; to a memory of a visit to a mercenary hypnotherapist in Melbourne's Swanston Street – until, through the suggestion of a Swedish friend with an interest in ancient Sumerian mythology – "who calls himself Elk on odd days and Godflesh on even days. Don't ask why" – he finally arrives with a joyous heart at the Mesopotamian god MARU-TUKKU, "Master of the Arts of Protection".

If MARUTUKKU was my exquisite cryptographic good, of wit, effusive joy, ravishing pleasure and flattering hope; then where was the counter point? The figure to its ground – the sharper evil, the madness, the melancholy, the most cruel lassitudes and disgusts and the severest disappointments. Was Hume right?

Alas, he was. Assange, "on a cold and wintry night here in Melbourne", discovers in the 4000-year-old Babylonian tablets a reference to the supposedly secret eavesdropping intelligence agency in Maryland, the National Security Agency! It is a magnificently exuberant, bravura literary performance. Assange was not merely a talented code writer and computer geek. There was in him daring, wildness and a touch of genius. For a while he signed his emails not with his customary "Proff." but "Prof. Julian Assange".

Assange was by now a committed member of the free software movement, pioneered by Richard Stallman, whose aim was to regulate communication in cyberspace by software not by law. As members of the movement put it, freedom here meant free speech rather than free beer. The movement stressed democratic, collective contribution. Assange tended to be somewhat sceptical about the movement, on one occasion arguing that in reality usually one or two people did 80% of the work. Assange was nonetheless involved in the development of NetBSD, an open source computer operating system derived from the original Berkeley Software Distribution source code. Some of the slogans he invented to spruik its virtues can still be found on the internet. Here are three. "We put the OS in OrgaSm"; "Bits for Tits"; "More ports than a Norwegian crack whore" – all examples, as Assange now sees it, of his youthful "ribald humour".

By the time Assange was working on NetBSD he had been involved for several years with a movement known as the cypherpunks. It was the cypherpunks more than the free software movement who provided him with his political education. Although there are tens of thousands of articles on Julian Assange in the world's newspapers and magazines, no mainstream journalist so far has grasped the critical significance of the cypherpunks movement to Assange's intellectual development and the origin of WikiLeaks.

*

The cypherpunks emerged from a meeting of minds in late 1992 in the Bay Area of San Francisco. Its founders were Eric Hughes, a brilliant Berkeley mathematician; Timothy C. May, an already wealthy, former chief scientist at Intel who had retired at the age of thirty-four; and John Gilmore, another already retired and wealthy computer scientist – once number five at Sun Micro-systems – who had co-founded an organisation to advance the cause of cyberspace freedom, the Electronic Frontier Foundation. They created a small group, which met monthly in Gilmore's office at a business he had created, Cygnus. At one of the early meetings of the group, an editor at *Mondo 2000*, Jude Milhon, jokingly called them cypherpunks, a play on cyberpunk, the "hi-tech, low-life" science-fiction genre. The name stuck. It soon referred to a vibrant emailing list, created shortly after the first meeting, which had grown to 700 by 1994 and perhaps 2000 by 1997 with by then up to a hundred postings per day. It also referred to a distinctive sub-culture – eventually there were cypherpunk novels, *Snowcrash*, *Cryptonomicon*, *Indecent Communications*; a cypherpunk porno film, *Cryptic Seduction*; and even a distinctive cypherpunk dress: broad-brimmed black hats. Most importantly, however, it referred to a political–ideological crusade.

At the core of the cypherpunk philosophy was the belief that the great question of politics in the age of the internet was whether the state would strangle individual freedom and privacy through its capacity for electronic surveillance or whether autonomous individuals would eventually undermine and even destroy the state through their deployment of electronic weapons newly at hand. Many cypherpunks were optimistic that in the battle for the future of humankind – between the State and the Individual – the individual would ultimately triumph. Their optimism was based on developments in intellectual history and computer software: the invention in the mid-1970s of public-key cryptography by Whitfield Diffie and Martin Hellman, and the creation by Phil Zimmerman in the early 1990s of a program known as PGP, "Pretty Good Privacy". The seminal historian of codes, David Kahn, argued that the Diffie–Hellman invention represented the most important development in cryptography since the Renaissance. Zimmerman's PGP program democratised their invention and provided individuals, free of cost, with access to public-key cryptography and thus the capacity to communicate with others in near-perfect privacy. Although George Orwell's *Nineteen Eighty-Four* was one of the cypherpunks' foundational texts, because of the combination of public-key cryptography and PGP software, they tended to believe that in the coming battle between Big Brother and Winston Smith, the victor might be Winston Smith.

At the time the cypherpunks formed, the American government strongly opposed the free circulation of public-key cryptography. It feared that making it available would strengthen the hands of the espionage agencies of America's enemies abroad and of terrorists, organised criminals, drug dealers and pornographers at home. For the cypher-punks, the question of whether cryptography would be freely available would determine the outcome of the great battle of the age. Their most important practical task was to write software that would expand the oppor-tunities for anonymous communication made possible by public-key cryptography. One of the key projects of the cypherpunks was "remailers", software systems that made it impossible for governments to trace the passage from sender to receiver of encrypted email traffic. Another key project was "digital cash", a means of disguising financial trans-actions from the state.

Almost all cypherpunks were anarchists who regarded the state as the enemy. Most but not all were anarchists of the Right, or in American parlance, libertarians, who supported laissez-faire capitalism. The most authoritative political voice among the majority libertarian cypherpunks was Tim May, who, in 1994, composed a vast, truly remarkable document, "Cyphernomicon". May called his system crypto-anarchy. He regarded crypto-anarchy as the most original contribution to political ideology of contemporary times. May thought the state to be the source of evil in history. He envisaged the future as an Ayn Rand utopia of autonomous individuals dealing with each other as they pleased. Before this future arrived, he advocated tax avoidance, insider trading, money laundering, markets for information of all kinds, including military secrets, and what he called assassination markets not only for those who broke contracts or committed serious crime but also for state officials and

the politicians he called "Congressrodents".
He recognised that in his future world only
elites with control over technology would
prosper. No doubt "the clueless 95%" –
whom he described as "inner city breeders"
and as "the unproductive, the halt and the
lame" – "would suffer, but that is only just".
May acknowledged that many cypherpunks
would regard these ideas as extreme. He also
acknowledged that, while the overwhelming majority of cypherpunks were, like him,
anarcho-capitalist libertarians, some were
strait-laced Republicans, left-leaning liber-
als, Wobblies or even Maoists. Neither fact
concerned him. The cypherpunks formed a
house of many rooms. The only thing they all
shared was an understanding of the political
significance of cryptography and the will-
ingness to fight for privacy and unfettered
freedom in cyberspace.

Like an inverse Marxist, Tim May tended

to believe that the inexorable expansion of private cryptography made the victory of crypto-anarchism inevitable. A new "balance of power between individuals and larger entities" was already emerging. He predicted with some confidence "the end of governments as we know them". Another even more extreme cypherpunk of the libertarian Right, Jim Bell, like an inverse Leninist, thought that history might need a push. In mid-1995, drawing upon May's recommendation of assassination markets, he began a series explaining his "revolutionary idea", which he called "Assassination Politics". These were perhaps the most notorious and controversial postings in the history of the cypherpunks list. Bell devised a system in which citizens could contribute towards a lottery fund for the assassination of particular government officials. The prize would go to the person who correctly predicted the date of the death. The winner would obviously be the official's murderer. However, through the use of public-key cryptography, remailers and digital cash, from the time they entered the competition to the collection of the prize no one except the murderer would be aware of their identity. Under the rubric "tax is theft" all government officials and politicians were legitimate targets of assassination. Journalists would begin to ask of politicians, "Why should you not be killed?" As prudence would eventually dictate that no one take the job, the state would simply wither away. Moreover, as assassination lotteries could be extended across borders, no leader would again risk taking their people to war. Eventually, through the idea of the assassination lottery, then, not only would the era of anarchy arise across the globe, the condition of permanent peace humankind had long dreamt of would finally come to pass.

Bell ended his 20,000 word series of postings with these words. "Is all this wishful thinking? I really don't know!" A year or so later he was arrested on tax avoidance charges.

Julian Assange informed me he joined the cypherpunks email list in late 1993 or early 1994. There were many reasons Assange was likely to be attracted to it. As his encounter with Richard Lowenstein had revealed, he was interested in the connection between privacy and encrypted communication. Even before his arrest he had feared the intrusion into his life of the totalitarian surveillance state. An atmosphere of paranoia pervaded the cypherpunks list. Assange believed that he had been wrongly convicted of what he called a "victimless crime". The struggle against victimless crimes – the right to consume pornography, to communicate in cyberspace anonymously, to distribute cryptographic software freely – was at the centre of the cypherpunks' political agenda. Moreover the atmosphere of the list was free-wheeling – racism, sexism, homophobia were common. Not only Tim May believed that political correctness had turned Americans into "a nation of sheep". On the cypherpunks list no one would disapprove of "The Dan Farmer rag". Yet there was probably more to it than all this. Cypherpunks saw themselves as Silicon Valley Masters of the Universe. It must have been more than a little gratifying for a self-educated antipodean computer hacker, who had not even completed high school, to converse on equal terms with professors of mathematics, whiz-kid businessmen and some of the leading computer code-writers in the world.

Julian Assange contributed to the cypherpunks list until June 2002. As it happens, almost all his interventions have been placed on the internet. On the basis of what historians call primary evidence, the mind and character of Julian Assange can be seen at the time of his obscurity.

The first thing that becomes clear is the brashness. Over a technical dispute, he writes: "[B]oy are you a dummy." When someone asks for assistance in compiling a public list of hackers with handles, names, email addresses, Assange responds: "Are you on this list of morons?" In a dispute over religion and intolerance one cypherpunk had written: "Because those being hatefully intolerant have the 'right' beliefs as to what the Bible says. Am I a racist if I don't also include an example from the Koran?" "No, just an illiterate," Assange replied. Following a savaging from Assange for total computer incompetence, a hapless cypherpunk pointed out that he has been writing code since the age of fourteen. If one thing is clear from the cypherpunks list, it is that the young Julian

Assange did not suffer those he regarded as fools gladly.

In his posts there is humour, although often it is sarcastic. In one of his earliest interventions Assange has read about the arrest of someone caught with diesel fuel and fertiliser. "Looks like I've just been placed into the ranks of the pyro-terrorist. Golly, Deisel [sic] fuel. Gosh, Fertilizer. Ma, other items." Some posts reflect his faith in the theory of evolution. Assange forwarded an article about the role played by the CIA in supplying crack gangs in Los Angeles. A cypherpunk responded: "I wish they'd get back to the business, but add an overt poison to the product. Clean out the shit from the cities. Long live Darwinism." "Darwinism is working as well as it ever was. You may not like it but shit is being selected for," Assange shot back. Other posts reflect his recent life experiences. Assange had helped

Victoria Police break a paedophile ring in 1993. On the cypherpunks list he defended the circulation of child pornography on the internet on the grounds that it would cut the need for new production and make it easier for police to capture paedophiles. In another post he expressed deep anger at perceived injustice regarding those with whom he identifies – convicted hackers. One, Tsutomu Shimamura, had not only played a role in the hunting down of a notorious American fellow hacker, Kevin Mitnick (known personally to Assange through his research for *Underground*), but had even co-authored a book about it, *Takedown*. "This makes me ill. Tsutomu, when Mitnick cracks will you dig up his grave and rent his hands out as ash trays?" Assange also posted on the reports of violence against another hacker, Ed Cummings a.k.a. Bernie S, imprisoned in the US. "I was shocked. I've had some dealings with the SS... Those that abuse their power and inflict grave violence on others must be held accountable and their crimes deplored and punished in the strongest manner. Failure to do so merely creates an environment where such behaviour becomes predominant."

Already there are qualities in Assange's postings that are unusual in the standard cypherpunk. One is a fascination with language. Assange invented with Richard Jones a software program that created anagrams. The deepest institutional enemy of the cypherpunks was the National Security Agency. Assange put the name into his computer. Among the anagrams that emerged were: "National Anti-Secrecy Guy"; "Secret Analytic Guy Union"; "Caution Laying Any Secret"; "Insane, ugly, acne atrocity"; and, Assange's apparent favourite: "National Gay Secrecy Unit". He was also interested in what he described as "tracking language drift; i.e.

the relative change in word frequency on the internet as time goes by". He informed the cypherpunks that he had just discovered that in a "10 billion word corpus" the following frequency occurred:

God – 2,177,242
America – 2,178,046
Designed – 2,181,106
Five – 2,189,194
December – 2,190,028

His eccentricity would also have been obvious after a member of the "firewalls" list forwarded his MARUTUKKU fantasia to cypherpunks.

Where did Assange stand with regard to the radical cypherpunks agenda of Tim May? This question is best answered in two parts. On the question of cryptographic freedom and hostility towards the surveillance state and its chief embodiment – the National Security Agency – Assange was, if anything, even more absolute and extreme than May. In September 1996, Esther Dyson, the chair of the lobby group for freedom in cyberspace, the Electronic Frontier Foundation, was quoted in the *Los Angeles Times* as being in favour of certain extremely limited restrictions on internet anonymity. On the cypherpunks list a furious controversy, called "The Esther Dyson Fuss", broke out. Some cypherpunks defended Dyson on the ground that she had every right to argue a more nuanced position and that it was anyhow healthy for individuals to speak their mind. May vehemently disagreed. The issue was not her freedom of speech. A critical moment in the battle between freedom and surveillance had arrived. Dyson had defected to the enemy camp. Assange went further. He launched a stinging ad hominem attack.

Examining in detail Dyson's interests it appears she maintains a sizeable and longstanding interest in Eastern European technology companies. She is also very far to the right of the political spectrum (rampant capitalist would be putting it mildly). She also speaks Russian. I'm not saying she's been working for the CIA for the past decade, but I would be very surprised if the CIA has not exerted quite significant pressure . . . in order to bring her into their folds during that time period.

"At least you don't accuse me of being a Communist," Dyson responded. "For the record, I am not a tool of the CIA nor have they pressured me, but there's no reason for you to believe me." Later, Assange informed me, they became friends. However, when Assange was in trouble last year Dyson wrote a piece on the Salon website arguing that even unpleasant characters need to be defended.

A month or so after September 11 a controversy broke out on the cypherpunks list over the report of a civilised discussion about increased FBI surveillance over internet communications between Mitch Kapor, a co-founder and former board member of the Electronic Frontier Foundation, and Stu Baker, an attorney who had once been employed by the National Security Agency. Some cypherpunks had some sympathy for Kapor's moderation. Even they recognised that with September 11 something major had occurred. One pointed out, in addition, that Stu Baker was "a gun-for-hire, not a doctrinaire blinders-on true believer for either the surveillance enthusiasts or privacy freaks". This was too much for Assange:

> Stu is a well known NSA zealot. The
> only reason there's a bridge between

Kapor and Baker is due to the cavernous ravine that lays [sic] between them. Kapor is now apparently half-way across, following Stu's silently beckoning finger, fearfully running from the sounds of angels [sic] wings; fooled into believing that they lie behind and not ahead of him.

From beginning to end Assange was, in short, a hardline member of the tendency among the cypherpunks that Tim May called the "rejectionists", an enemy of those who displayed even the slightest tendency to compromise on the question of Big Brother and the surveillance state.

On another question, however, Assange was at the opposite end of the cypherpunks spectrum from Tim May. At no stage did Assange show sympathy for the anarchocapitalism of the cypherpunks mainstream which, as he explained to me, he regarded as "naive" about "the state tendencies of corporatism". In October 1996, a prominent cypherpunk, Duncan Frissell, claimed that in the previous fiscal year the American government had seized more tax than any government in history. Assange pointed out that, as the US was the world's largest economy and its GDP had grown in the previous year, this was a ridiculous statement designed to be deceptive. In October 2001, Declan McCullagh expressed "surprise" when a "critique of laissez-faire capitalism" appeared on the cypherpunks list "of all places". Assange replied:

> Declan, Declan.
> Put away your straw man ... Nobel economic laureates have been telling us for years to be careful about idealised market models ... This years [sic]

Nobel for Economics won by George A.
Akerlof, A. Michael Spence and Joseph
E. Stiglitz "for their analysis of markets
with assymmetric [sic] information"
is typical. You don't need a Nobel to
realize that the relationship between a
large employer and employee is brutally
assymmetric [sic] ... To counter this sort
of assymetery. [sic] Employees naturally
start trying to collectivise to increase
their information processing and bar-
gaining power. That's right. UNIONS
Declan. Those devious entities that
first world companies and governments
have had a hand in suppressing all over
the third world by curtailing freedom
of association, speech and other basic
political rights we take for granted.

Assange was, then, an absolutist crypto-
anarchist but one who leant decidedly to

the Left. Mainstream cypherpunks did not defend trade unions or speak negatively of "rampant capitalists" and positively of "human rights activists". He was an electronic but not an economic libertarian.

There is also evidence that Assange was increasingly repelled by the corrosive cynicism common in cypherpunks ranks. Something in his spirit seems to have changed after his trial and the writing of his MARUTUKKU mythology. From 1997 to 2002 Julian Assange accompanied all his cypherpunks postings with this beautiful passage from Antoine de Saint-Exupéry: "If you want to build a ship, don't drum up people together to collect wood and don't assign them tasks and work, but rather teach them to long for the endless immensity of the sea." On one occasion in July 1999 William H. Geiger III presented standard Ayn Rand Objectivist praise of human selfishness.

"Everyone is a predator out to advance their own agenda at the expence [sic] of others. Tim is just more honest than most about it." Assange replied with a defence of altruism, for Objectivists an evil.

> No ... Everyone maybe self-interested, but some are self-interested in a way that is healthy (to you, or the people you care about), some in a way which is benign, and some in a manner that is pernicious. It is important to distinguish between these different behaviours and support or undermine them accordingly.

On another occasion, a cypherpunk suggested that in the great struggle for privacy and against censorship ordinary people could not give a damn. Perhaps with Tim May's contempt for "the clueless 95%" in his mind, in March 2002, in what was one of his final cypherpunks postings, Assange responded: "The 95% of the population which comprise the flock have never been my target and neither should they be yours; it's the 2.5% at either end of the normal that I find in my sights, one to be cherished and the other to be destroyed." Already he seems to have imagined the future as a struggle to the death between autocratic elites and electronic freedom fighters. Increasingly, Assange began to mock Tim May. Many thought of May as an anti-Semite, with good reason. In November 2001, when May used a quote from a cypherpunk fellow traveller, David Friedman (Milton's son), Assange emailed: "Quoting Jews again, Tim?"

Julian Assange was a regular contributor to the cypherpunks mailing list particularly before its decline in late 1997 following a meltdown over the question of the possible moderation of the list – censorship! – and

the departure of John Gilmore. The cypherpunks list clearly mattered to him deeply.
Shortly before his travels in 1998, Assange
asked whether anyone could send him a
complete archive of the list between 1992
and the present time. While commentators
have comprehensively failed to see the significance of the cypherpunks in shaping the
thought of Julian Assange, this is something
insiders to the movement understand. When
Jeanne Whalen from the *Wall Street Journal*
approached John Young of Cryptome in
August last year, he advised her to read the
Assange cypherpunk postings he had just
placed on the internet, and also Tim May's
"Cyphernomicon". "This background has not
been explored in the WikiLeaks saga. And
WikiLeaks cannot be understood without
it." Likewise, in his mordant online article
on WikiLeaks and Assange, the influential
cyberpunk novelist and author of *The Hacker*

Crackdown Bruce Sterling wrote: "At last – at long last – the homemade nitroglycerin in the old cypherpunks blast shack has gone off."

*

In 2003 Julian Assange seems to have considered living a more conventional life. He went to the University of Melbourne to study mainly mathematics and physics. As a student of mathematics his results were mixed but generally mediocre. This can hardly be explained by lack of talent. No one worked more closely with Assange than Suelette Dreyfus. "A geek friend of his once described Assange as having an IQ 'in excess of 170'," she wrote in the *Sydney Morning Herald* of 12 December 2010. "I suspect this could be true." Assange claimed that he became disillusioned with the applied maths department when he discovered its members were working with defence authorities in the US on a military bulldozer adapted to desert conditions known as "The Grizzly Plough". He also claimed that visits to the ANU were thoroughly dispiriting. On one occasion he represented University of Melbourne students at a competition. "At the prize ceremony, the head of ANU physics motioned to us and said, 'you are the cream of Australian physics.' I looked around and thought, 'Christ Almighty I hope he's wrong.'" On another occasion he saw 900 senior physicists in Canberra proudly carrying bags with the logo of the Defence Science and Technology Organisation. He described them as "snivelling fearful conformists of woefully, woefully inferior character".

Perhaps there were other reasons for dissatisfaction. By 2004 Assange had reached the elevated position of vice-president of the students' Mathematics and Statistics Society and chief organiser of their Puzzle

Hunt—a quiz leading the winner to $200 of buried treasure. He described his role as "plot/script, general nonsense, Abstract(ion), Caesar Cipher, Disc, Platonic, Score, Surstro:mming". Assange explained that he "invented/founded the competition to improve the intellectual climate in Australia." Nonetheless, organising a puzzle hunt was a somewhat less engrossing ambition than planning world revolution. And towards the end of his studies this was exactly what he was doing. A female friend provided the journalist Nikki Barrowclough with a vivid portrait of the atmosphere of a share house close-by the University of Melbourne that Assange lived in at this time.

> There were beds everywhere, she says.
> There was even a bed in the kitchen.
> This woman slept on a mattress in
> Assange's room, and says she would

sometimes wake up in the middle of
the night to find him still glued to his
computer. He frequently forgot to eat or
sleep, wrote mathematical formulas all
over the walls and the doors, and used
only red light bulbs in his room – on the
basis that early man, if waking suddenly,
would see only the gentle light of the
campfire, and fall asleep again.

Between July 2006 and August 2007 – the
period when WikiLeaks was being planned
and actualised – Julian Assange maintained a
blog at IQ.ORG, some of which he collected
under the title "Selected Correspondence".
The correspondence can still be found on the
internet. Because of its existence, a reason-
ably detailed map of his mind at the age of
thirty-five and at the moment of WikiLeaks'
creation is available. Strangely enough, even
though there are now some 27 million Google

entries on Assange, so far as I am aware no one has offered an analysis.

The blog reveals a young man of unusual intellectual range, ambition and curiosity. As expected, there are references to cypher-punks and his work as a code-writer in the free software movement. Assange writes of his loathing for the "'everything which is not explicitly permitted is denied' security types" who "make concurrent salutes to the Fuhrer, Baal and Jack Straw". He explains why as one of the committed developers of NetBSD he has refused to sign a proposed contract: "The contract as well as being an instrument of the state is written in the demeaning language of the corporate state. It should have been written in the language of our programmer world." Some entries, such as his defence of altruism, are familiar to those who have followed his postings on the cypherpunks list. Many others have the range and also eccentricity revealed in his MARUTUKKU performance. There are abstract speculations on philosophy, mathematics, neuroscience, human physiology, the law, history and sociology.

There are also very striking and revealing extracts. One is from a Buddhist text from 500 BC, *Ajita Kesakambali*, in defence of materialism. "The words of those who speak of existence after death are false, empty chatter. With the break-up of the body, the wise and the foolish are alike annihilated, destroyed." Another is a wonderful story from the Nazi concentration camp. A Jewish inmate can save his daughter if he chooses which eye of his guard is glass. He chooses the left eye, correctly. His guard asks how he knew. "'I'm sorry,' trembled Moshe, 'but the left eye looks at me with a kindly gleam.'" Assange has great interest in the history of European totalitarianism. One extract is a poem – "bad … but elevated by its monumental context" – about the atom bomb spies Ethel and Julius Rosenberg: "Even so, we did what we believed in: / Treason, yes, perhaps, but with good cause." There is also a long extract from an article about the problems besetting those possessing super-high IQs, such as the unfulfilled genius William James Sidis. It concludes with these words: "And so we see that the explanation for the Sidis tragedy is simple. Sidis was a feral child; a true man born into a world filled with animals – a world filled with us." It is not difficult to understand why this article interested him.

Many blog entries are personal. When Daniel Domscheit-Berg released his memoir, *Inside WikiLeaks*, there was excitement around the globe at his claim that Assange had boasted about fathering several children, something Assange fiercely denies. About one child at least there can be no doubt.

On his blog, Assange includes a photo of a bonneted baby under the title "Those Eyes" with the caption, "All the pink ribbons in the world can't hide them." She is his new daughter. Another entry referred obliquely to his mother's organisation of "The Great Bikini March" against Sheikh Hilaly, who had recently compared women who dressed scantily to "uncovered meat". Some entries about women fleetingly encountered are awkward in a Mills & Boon kind of way. "A lovely girl I knew … stood for a moment fully clothed in her shower before letting the wind and rain buffet her body as she made her tremulous approach to my door and of course I could not turn her away." One – Assange's study of the etymology of the word "cad" – seems to me rather sinister. "Caddie or cadet used to denote the passenger of a horse-coach picked up for personal profit by the driver … So a 'cad' is a man who picks up women, profits from them and leaves them by the road side ... Such romantic etymology is enough to make a man want to don his oilskin and mount his horse with whip and smile at the ready." The coldness of tone here, which Assange ascribes to his taste for "black humour", is striking precisely because other passages in the correspondence are so tender. Assange writes of meeting Antony, a country kid he had known since they were both fourteen, at a mental health centre in East Ringwood. "His smile was shaky but characteristic. His physical edges rounded off by weight gain and his imagination dulled ... His limbs and jaw gently shuddered with some frequency." Assange visited him later still at a psychiatric hospital. "When I asked about the cause of his shaking, suggesting a dopamine antagonist, he said, 'No ... If you look closely you'll notice a number of people around here acting the same way. Julian ...

we're all doing the Mont Park shuffle.'"

What is most important about the correspondence, however, is that in it we can hear
for the first time Julian Assange's distinctive political voice. As a former cypherpunk
crypto-anarchist the enemy for him is,
unsurprisingly, that abstraction he calls the
State. "Where words have power to change,
the state tries hard to trap, burn or blank
them, such is its fear of their power." The
state represents the principle of "mendacity".
"The state does what it can get away with."
True understanding requires the individual
"to know the state for what it really is". Yet,
unlike most of his fellow cypherpunks, by
now Assange unambiguously extends his idea
of the state to big business. In thinking about
the US, in one blog entry, he asks: "What
kinds of states are giant corporations?" He
answers in the following way. As executive
power is wielded by a central committee; as

there is unaccountable single-party rule; as there is no freedom of speech or association, and "pervasive surveillance of movement and electronic communication", what then do you have in that federation of giant corporations that control the US? What else but a "United Soviet of America". Assange is a profound anti-communist. But he regards power in Western society as belonging to political and economic elites offering ordinary people nothing more nourishing than a counterfeit conception of democracy and a soul-destroying consumption culture.

Assange's selected correspondence is addressed to a small coterie of followers. It involves a revolutionary call to arms. "If we can only live once, then let it be a daring adventure that draws on all our powers... Let our grandchildren delight to find the start of our stories in their ears but the endings all around in their wandering eyes." Assange seems not particularly interested in future political institutions or in economic arrangements. The revolution he speaks about is moral. He believes that individual action can re-fashion the world. The state may do "what it can get away with" but it does "what we let it get away with" and even "what we let ourselves get away with, for we, in our interactions with others, form the state". Over the whole selected correspondence there is a quotation from the German–Jewish revolutionary anarchist Gustav Landauer, beaten to death by right-wing troops after the Munich soviet experiment of 1919. "The state is a condition, a certain relationship between human beings, a mode of behaviour. We destroy it by contracting other relationships, by behaving differently toward one another ... We are the state and we shall continue to be the state until we have created the institutions that form a real community and society of men." The question is how new institutions can be formed.

In the struggle to create a truly human society, Assange warns his interlocutors not to believe they can think globally but act locally. This is an illusion. Action must be taken on a truly global scale. He is also witheringly contemptuous of those he calls "the typical shy intellectual".

> This type is often of a noble heart,
> wilted by fear of conflict with authority.
> The power of their intellect and noble
> instincts may lead them to a courageous
> position, where they see the need to
> take up arms, but their instinctive fear
> of authority then motivates them to find
> rationalizations to avoid conflict.

For Assange the central political virtue is courage. One of his favourite sayings is:

"Courage is contagious." He attributes it to the Pentagon Papers whistleblower Daniel Ellsberg. In fact it was coined by the evangelist Billy Graham. Assange's politics are also generational. "Perhaps as an old man I will take great comfort in pottering around in a lab and gently talking to students in the summer evening and will accept suffering with insouciance. But not now; men in their prime, if they have convictions are tasked to act on them."

For Assange the great moving forces in history are the need for Love and the thirst for Truth. In his final piece in the selected correspondence, Assange admits that often "outcomes are treated with more reverence than Truth".

> Yet just as we feel all hope is lost and we sink into the miasma, back to the shadow world of ghosts and gods, a

miracle arises, everywhere before the
direction of self interest is known,
people yearn to see where its compass
points and then they hunger for truth
with passion and beauty and insight . . .
Here then is the truth to set them
free. Free from the manipulations and
constraints of the mendacious. Free to
choose their path, free to remove the
ring from their noses, free to look up
into the infinite void and choose wonder
over whatever gets them through. And
before this feeling to cast blessings on
the profits and prophets of truth . . . on
the Voltaires, the Galileos and Principias
of truth, on the Gutenbergs, Marconis
and Internets of truth, those serial killers
of delusion, those brutal, driven and
obsessed miners of reality, smashing,
smashing, smashing every rotten edifice
until all is ruins and the seeds of the new.

But how will the rotten edifice be smashed? On 22 November 2006 Assange provides a link to a paper. He tells his coterie of readers: "No. Don't skip to the good stuff. This is the good stuff." He is pointing them to the central theoretical breakthrough that led to WikiLeaks.

Julian Assange published this paper twice, the first time on 10 November 2006 under the title "State and Terrorist Conspiracies", the second time, in more developed form, on 3 December under the title "Conspiracy as Governance". Stripped of its inessential mathematical gobbledegook, its argument goes like this. The world is at present dominated by the conspiratorial power of authoritarian governments and big business corporations. As President Theodore Roosevelt understood, behind "ostensible governments", there exists "an invisible government owing no allegiance and acknowledging no responsibility to the people. To destroy this invisible government, to befoul this unholy alliance between corrupt business and corrupt politics is the first task of statesmanship." Authoritarian governments and corporations maintain and entrench their power through a conspiracy. For Assange the conspiracy involves the maintenance of a network of links between the conspirators, some vital, some less so. Conspiracies naturally provoke resistance. Among revolutionaries of earlier generations resistance has involved the attempt to break the links between the leaders of the conspiracy by "assassination . . . killing, kidnapping, blackmailing, or otherwise marginalising or isolating some of the conspirators they were connected to". Such methods are no longer appropriate. "The act of assassination – the targeting of visible individuals, is the result of mental inclinations honed for the pre-literate societies in which our species evolved." The new generation of revolutionaries "must think beyond those who have gone before us, and discover technological changes that embolden us with ways to act in which our forebears could not".

Contemporary conspiracies rely on un-restricted information flow to adapt to and control their environments. Conspirators need to be able to speak freely to each other and to disarm resistance by spreading disin-formation among the people they control, something they presently very successfully achieve. Conspirators who have control over information flow are infinitely more pow-erful than those who do not. Drawing on a passage from Lord Halifax in which polit-ical parties are described as "conspiracies against the rest of the nation", Assange asks his readers to imagine what would happen in the struggle between the Republican and Democratic parties in the US "if one of these parties gave up their mobile phones, fax and email correspondence – let alone the computer systems that manage their subscribes [sic], donors, budgets, polling, call centres and direct mail campaigns". He asks them to think of the conspiracy as a living organism, "a beast with arteries and veins whose blood may be thickened and slowed until it falls, stupefied; unable to sufficiently comprehend and control the forces in its environment". Rather than attacking the conspiracy by assassinating its leading members, he believes it can be "throttled" by cutting its information flows. "Later," he promises, "we will see how new technology and insights into the psychological motivations of conspirators can give us practical methods for preventing or reducing important communication between authoritarian conspirators, foment strong resistance to authoritarian planning and create powerful incentives for more humane forms of governance."

The promise is fulfilled in a blog entry of 31 December 2006. Here he outlines finally the idea at the core of the WikiLeaks strategy.

> The more secretive or unjust an organization is, the more leaks induce fear and paranoia in its leadership and planning coterie. This must result in minimization of efficient internal communications mechanisms (an increase in cognitive "secrecy tax") and consequent system-wide cognitive decline resulting in decreased ability to hold onto power as the environment demands adaptation.
>
> Hence in a world where leaking is easy, secretive or unjust systems are nonlinearly hit relative to open, just systems. Since unjust systems, by their nature induce opponents, and in many

places barely have the upper hand,
leaking leaves them exquisitely vulnerable to those who seek to replace them
with more open forms of governance.

There is a link between Assange's cypherpunks period and the theory behind
WikiLeaks. Assange was a contributor to
the cypherpunks list at the time when Jim
Bell's "Assassination Politics" was being
hotly discussed. There is evidence that
Assange was intrigued by the idea. In January
1998 he had come upon an advertisement
for a prize – "Scoop the Grim Reaper. Who
Will Live? Who Will Die?" – which was to
be awarded to the person who guessed on
what dates certain Hollywood celebrities
would die. "Anyone noticed this before?"
Assange posted the advertisement on the
cypherpunks list under the heading: "Jim . . .
Bell . . . lives . . . on . . . in . . . Hollywood".

Although Assange assured me he was not thinking about "Assassination Politics" at the time he was inventing WikiLeaks, there are similarities between Bell's thought and Assange's. Like Bell, Assange was possessed by a simple "revolutionary idea" about how to create a better world. As with Bell, the idea emerged from reflection upon the political possibilities created by untraceable anonymous communication, through the use of remailers and unbreakable public-key cryptography. The differences are also clear. Unlike with Bell, the revolution Assange imagined would be non-violent. The agent of change would not be the assassin but the whistleblower. The method would not be the bullet but the leak.

In arriving at this position, Assange had drawn together different personal experiences. It was as a "frontier hactivist" and as "Australia's first electronic publisher" that he had become interested in the political potency of leaks. From his cypherpunk days he had become engaged in discussions about the political possibilities of untraceable encrypted communication. And from his involvement in the free software movement he had seen what collective democratic intellectual enterprise might achieve. In essence, his conclusion was that world politics could be transformed by staunching the flow of information among corrupt power elites by making them ever more fearful of insider leaks. He believed he could achieve this by establishing an organisation that would allow whistleblowers from all countries to pass on their information, confident that their identities would not be able to be discovered. He proposed that his organisation would then publish the information for the purpose of collective analysis so as to empower oppressed populations across the globe.

There are few original ideas in politics. In the creation of WikiLeaks, Julian Assange was responsible for one.

*

In late 2006 Assange sought a romantic partner through OKCupid using the name of Harry Harrison. Under the heading, "What am I doing with my life?", he answered: "directing a consuming, dangerous human rights project which is, as you might expect, male-dominated". Under the heading, "I spend a lot of time thinking about", he answered: "Changing the world through passion, inspiration and trickery". There was something distinctly Walter Mittyish about it all. Under the informal leadership of Julian Assange, a group of mainly young men, without resources and linked only by computers, now began to implement their plans for a peaceful global political revolution.

On 4 October 2006 Assange registered
the domain name "WikiLeaks.org" in the
US. He called it WikiLeaks because he had
been immensely impressed by the success of
the Wikipedia experiment, where 3 million
entries had been contributed through the
input of a worldwide virtual community.
As he put it, WikiLeaks would be to leaks
what Wikipedia was to the encyclopedia.
Strangely and perhaps revealingly, it was registered under the names of two fathers, his
biological one, John Shipton, and his cypherpunk political one, John Young, a New York
architect who ran the intelligence leak
website Cryptome, which could be seen as
WikiLeaks' predecessor. Assange explained
his request for assistance to Young like this:

> You knew me under another name
> from cypherpunks days. I am involved
> in a project that you may have a feeling

for ... The project is a mass document
leaking project that requires someone
with backbone to hold the .org domain
registration ... We expect the domain to
come under the usual political and legal
pressure. The policy for .org requires
that registrants [sic] details not be false
or misleading. It would be an easy play
to cancel the domain unless someone
were willing to stand up and claim to be
the registrant.

The choice of Young reveals something
about Assange. For Young was undoubtedly
the most militant security cypherpunk of all,
who had published on his website an aerial
photo of Dick Cheney's hideout bunker, a
photograph of the home of Fox News's Bill
O'Reilly, and the names of 276 British and
some 600 Japanese intelligence agents and
2619 CIA "sources". Young was also Jim

Bell's greatest champion. After Bell's arrest and imprisonment, Young nominated him for the Chrysler Award for Innovation in Design. Bell had, he argued in his nomination, contributed "an imaginative and sophisticated prospective for improving governmental accountability by way of a scheme for anonymous, untraceable political assassination".

Serious work on the establishment of WikiLeaks began in December 2006. One of the first tasks was to decide upon a logo. Before opting for the hourglass, the WikiLeaks team thought seriously about a mole breaking through a wall above which stood three sinister authoritarian figures, arms folded. Another early task was to put together an advisory board. The first person he wanted was Daniel Ellsberg. Assange explained the purpose of WikiLeaks and why he had been approached:

> We'd like your advice and we'd like you
> to form part of our political armor. The
> more armor we have, particularly in the
> form of men and women sanctified by
> age, history and class, the more we can
> act like brazen young men and get away
> with it.

Here was one generation speaking to another. A month after being contacted Ellsberg replied. "Your concept is terrific and I wish you the best of luck with it." He did not agree to join the board. Two leading cypherpunks were approached – the British computer security specialist Ben Laurie and one of the cypherpunks' founders, John Gilmore. Laurie became actively involved. Gilmore instead asked the Electronic Frontier Foundation he had also co-founded to help. Assange's old cypherpunk sparring partner, Danny O'Brien, now with the EFF,

offered to assist. Also approached not long
after were two Chinese Tiananmen Square
dissidents, a member of the Tibetan Association in Washington and Australian journalist
Phillip Adams. All agreed to join the board
of advisers and, then, most seem never to
have heard from WikiLeaks again.

What do the early internal documents
reveal about the charge that WikiLeaks was
an anti-American outfit posing as a freedom
of information organisation? In his invita-
tion to Gilmore, Assange had pledged that
WikiLeaks "will provide a catalyst that will
bring down government through stealth
everywhere, not least that of the Bushists". In
its first public statement, WikiLeaks argued
that "misleading leaks and misinformation
are already well placed in the mainstream
media ... an obvious example being the
lead-up to the Iraq war". And in an email
of 2 January 2007 Assange even argued that

WikiLeaks could advance by several years "the total annihilation of the current US regime and any other regime that holds its authority through mendacity alone". And yet, despite these statements, the evidence surrounding WikiLeaks' foundation makes it abundantly clear that anti-Americanism was not the primary driving force. Time and again, in its internal documents, it argued that its "roots are in dissident com- munities" and that its "primary targets are those highly oppressive regimes in China, Russia and central Eurasia". China is a special focus. One or more of WikiLeaks' inner coterie were Taiwanese hacking into Chinese government sources. At the time of its foundation, WikiLeaks claimed to have more than a million documents. Almost certainly almost all came from China. For this reason, WikiLeaks argued publicly that "a politically motivated legal attack on us would be seen as a grave error in western administrations". Concerning its targets, the formulation is precise. WikiLeaks has in its sights authoritarian governments, the increasingly authoritarian tendencies seen in the recent trajectory of the Western democracies, and the authoritarian nature of contemporary business corporations.

What then of the charge that WikiLeaks was a revolutionary organisation pretending to be concerned merely with reformist liberal issues such as exposure of corruption, open government and freedom of information and expression? The internal WikiLeaks documents show that the answer to this question is complex. At its foundation, Assange frequently argued that WikiLeaks' true nature did indeed need to be disguised. Because "freedom of information is a respected liberal value", Assange argued, "we may get some sympathy" but it would not last. Inevitably governments would try to crush WikiLeaks. But if the mask of moderation was maintained, at least for some time, opposition would be "limp wristed". A quotation from the Book of Isaiah, he believed, might be suitable "if we were to *front* as a Ploughshares [peace] organisation". To John Young he wrote: "We have the collective sources, personalities and learning to be, *or rather appear to be*, the reclusive ubermensch of the 4th estate." The emphases are mine. He also knew that if WikiLeaks was to prosper, and also to win support from philanthropic bodies such as the Soros Foundation, the hacker–cypherpunk origin of the inner circle needed to be disguised. "We expect difficult state lashback [sic] unless WikiLeaks can be given a sanctified frame ('center for human rights, democracy, good government and apple pie press freedom project' vs 'hackers strike again')." The key to WikiLeaks was that its true revolutionary ambitions and its moderate liberal public face would be difficult for opponents to disentangle. Open government and freedom of information were standard liberal values. However, as explained in the theory outlined in "Conspiracy as Governance", they were the values in whose name authoritarian structures would be undermined worldwide, through the drying up of information flows and a paralysing fear of insider leaks.

It was not only opponents who found it difficult to keep the public and private faces of WikiLeaks distinct. Despite those involved understanding the need for disguise, at its foundation the excitement was so palpable and the ambition so boundless that, when it was called upon to explain itself, the mask of apple pie liberal reformist moderation instantly fell away. On 3 January 2007 a small crisis arose when WikiLeaks' existence was prematurely revealed. Assange immediately put together a brilliant description of WikiLeaks for public release.

> Principled leaking has changed the course of human history for the better; it can alter the course of history in the present; it can lead to a better future... Public scrutiny of otherwise unaccountable and secretive institutions pressures them to act ethically. What official will chance a secret corrupt transaction when the public is likely to find out?... When the risks of embarrassment through openness and honesty increase, the tables are turned against conspiracy, corruption, exploitation and oppression...
>
> Instead of a couple of academic specialists, WL will provide a forum for the entire global community to examine any

document relentlessly for credibility,
plausibility, veracity and falsifiability . . .
WL may become the most powerful
intelligence agency on earth, an intelligence agency of the people . . . WL will
be an anvil at which beats the hammer
of the collective conscience of humanity . . . WL, we hope, will be a new star
in the political firmament of humanity.

Julian Assange recognised that the language
of what amounted to the WikiLeaks Manifesto might appear a little "overblown". He
recognised that it had about it too much the
flavour of "anarchy". But in general when it
was written he was pleased.

John Young was not. In early January 2007
he decided that WikiLeaks was a CIA-backed
fraud. "Fuck your cute hustle and disinformation campaign. Same old shit, working for
the enemy . . . Fuck 'em all." "We are going

to fuck them all. Chinese mostly but not entirely a feint," Assange cryptically replied. Young decided now to post all the WikiLeaks correspondence he had seen between early December 2006 and early January 2007 on his website. Later, in 2010, he published Assange's contributions to the cypherpunks list between 1995 and 2002. It is because of his baseless suspicion that the mind of Julian Assange and the intellectual origins of WikiLeaks are able to be understood.

*

In February 2007, Julian Assange travelled to Nairobi to attend the World Social Forum, a very large gathering of mainly left-wing human rights activists and NGOs. He stayed on in Kenya for several months, involved with anti-corruption forces but also fascinated and repelled by the world of superstition he encountered:

Here, in Africa there was a two page fold
out on the "Night Runner" plague. Plague?
Yes. Of people – typically old, who supposedly run around naked at night … tapping
on windows, throwing rocks on peoples
[sic] roofs, snapping twigs, rustling grass,
casting spells and getting lynched because
it's the "right thing to do".

Insofar as we can affect the world,
let it be to utterly eliminate guilt and
fear as a motivator of man and replace it
cell for cell with love of one another and
the passion of creation.

Assange was a true Enlightenment Man.

The next Social Forum was to be held
between 27 June and 4 July in Atlanta.
Assange wanted WikiLeaks volunteers to
attend. Emails he sent in early June can be
found on the internet. They provide the
clearest evidence of his political viewpoint

and strategic thinking at this time. In the first he assures his supporters that Wiki-Leaks' future is secure. "[T]he idea can't be stopped. It's everyone's now." Some people have apparently argued that WikiLeaks' idealism or "childlike naivety" is a weakness. He believes they are entirely wrong. "Naivety is unfailingly attractive when it adorns strength. People rush forward to defend and fight for individuals and organizations imbued with this quality." Confronted by it, "virtuous sophisticates" are "marooned". Some people are clearly worried that Wiki-Leaks will be captured by "the Left". Assange assures his followers they need not be concerned. In the US the problem is rather that WikiLeaks is seen as too close to the CIA and American foreign policy. In fact, "we'll take our torch to all." Some people have clearly expressed doubts about Social Forum types. Assange more than shares them. They are by and large "ineffectual pansies" who "specialize in making movies about themselves and throwing 'dialogue' parties ... with foundation money", while fantasising that "the vast array of functional cogs in brute inhumanity ... would follow their lead, clapping, singing and videotaping their way up Mt. Mostly Harmless". In Africa Assange has seen human rights fighters of real backbone. He warns his followers not to expect to find such people in the US. He quotes at length from Solzhenitsyn's 1979 Harvard address about the radical decline of "civic courage" in the West especially among the "ruling and intellectual elites". Nonetheless, to advance WikiLeaks' cause, the Social Forum – the world's biggest NGO "beach party" – matters. Assange anticipates that anti–Iraq War feeling will hold it together. Although WikiLeaks has so far concentrated on "the most closed governments", he explains that it is about to publish explosive material on American "involvement in Iraq and Afghanistan". He hopes that the anti-war movement will embrace these documents so that WikiLeaks can avoid the "retributive" blast from pro-war forces. It is vital to position itself "as everyone's friend". If anyone still needs it, this despatch is proof that Assange has a biting tongue, a mordant wit and a brilliant political mind.

It is obvious that by June 2007 several members of the Left had indeed gravitated to WikiLeaks. In Assange's view, this group were thinking of publishing commentary on leaked documents in a way that allowed their political bias to show. He sent a different email to them:

> OK, you guys need to keep the Progressive/Commie/Socialist agendas and rhetoric to yourselves or you're going to

go absolutely nowhere very, very fast.
Now, now, don't get your dander up: if I
can pass by gross mis-characterizations
of the existing world order as "capitalism" or "white supremacy", you can stay
calm and listen a minute.

WikiLeaks was in danger, he argued, of
being positioned either as a CIA front by
John Young types or as a same-old left-
wing outfit "preaching to the choir". All
partisanship would be lethal. WikiLeaks
needed to keep itself open to whistleblowers of all stripes – even "conservative and
religious types waking up to the fact that
they've been taken for a ride". "What you
need to strive for is the same level of objec-
tivity and analytical disinterest as the League
of Women Voters. No, even higher. Else I'll
be so disheartened that I'll lower myself to
government contracting work." This email is

not only illuminating from the point of view of WikiLeaks' grand strategy. It is also decisive as to his true political position. Assange might have been on the left of the spectrum by anarcho-capitalist cypherpunk standards but he was by no means a standard leftist. His politics were anti-establishment but genuinely beyond Left and Right.

Between 2007 and 2010 Assange's political thinking was shaped by two key ideas. The first, as we have seen, was that all authoritarian structures – both governments and corporations – were vulnerable to insider leaks. Fear would throttle information flows. Assange called this a "secrecy tax". Inevitably, he argued, because of this tax, governments and corporations with nothing to hide would triumph over their secretive, unjust conspiratorial competitors. This aspect of his politics amounted to a kind of political Darwinism, a belief not in the survival of the fittest but of the most transparent and most just. As an organisation that encouraged whistleblowers and published their documents, WikiLeaks was aiding and speeding up this process.

There was, however, another dimension of his politics that reflected his long association with the cypherpunks. Assange believed that, in the era of globalisation, laws determining communication were going to be harmonised. The world would either opt for a closed system akin to Chinese political secrecy and American intellectual property laws, or an open system found to some extent in Belgium and Sweden. Once more, Assange hoped that WikiLeaks was assisting a positive outcome to this struggle through its role as what he called a global publisher of last resort. If WikiLeaks could survive the attacks certain to be mounted by governments and corporations, the rights of human beings to communicate freely with each other without the intervention of governments would be entrenched. WikiLeaks was, according to this argument, the canary in the mine. Assange was taken with the famous Orwell quote. "He who controls the present controls the past and he who controls the past controls the future." The world was at a turning point. Either Big Brother would take control of the internet or an era of unprecedented freedom of communication would arrive.

Assange was by now in the habit of composing motivational emails for his volunteers. This is the message he sent them on 12 March 2008:

> Mankind has successfully adapted
> changes as monumental as electricity and
> the engine. It can also adapt to a world
> where state sponsored violence against
> the communications of consenting

adults is not only unlawful, but physically impossible. As knowledge flows across nations it is time to sum the great freedoms of every nation and not subtract them. It is time for the world as an international collective of communicating peoples to arise and say "here I am".

This might have come straight out of a cypherpunks manifesto. In the first weeks of 2010 Assange was involved in an ultimately successful political manoeuvre to turn Iceland into the world's first "data haven" with the most politically progressive anticensorship laws on Earth.

There was an aspect of WikiLeaks' work that was, through 2008 and 2009, beginning to trouble Assange. Although it was a peripatetic organisation with a small permanent staff, WikiLeaks had proven to be an outstanding success in attracting leaks and then publishing them. By late 2009 it had published documents concerning an Islamist assassination order from Somalia; massive corruption in Daniel arap Moi's Kenya; tax avoidance by the largest Swiss bank, Julius Baer; an oil spill in Peru, a nuclear accident in Iran and toxic chemical dumping by the Trafigura corporation off the Ivory Coast. Further, it had released the Guantanamo Bay operational manuals; secret film of dissent in Tibet; the emails of Sarah Palin; a suppressed report into an assassination squad operating in Kenya; American intelligence reports on the battle of Fallujah, and reports into the conditions in its jails; the Climategate emails; the internet censorship lists from Australia; and, finally, the loans book of the Icelandic bank Kaupthing. WikiLeaks had never been successfully sued, although Julius Baer had tried. None of the identities of the whistle-blowers who sought to conceal them had been uncovered. WikiLeaks had won awards from the *Economist*, in 2008, and from Amnesty International, in 2009. Assange believed that WikiLeaks' information had determined a Kenyan election. He knew that the publication of the loans book in Iceland had riveted the nation, especially after Kaupthing had brought down an injunction against the national broadcaster's evening television news. And yet, as his internal communications make clear, he was puzzled and appalled by the world's indifference to his leaks.

Assange had once regarded WikiLeaks as the people's intelligence agency. In January 2007 he sincerely believed that when WikiLeaks published commentary on the Somalia assassination order document it would be "very closely collaboratively analysed by hundreds of Wikipedia editors" and by "thousands of refugees from the Somali, Ethiopian and Chinese expat communities".

This simply had not happened. Commentary by the people on material produced by their intelligence agency never would. He had once hoped for engaged analysis from the blogosphere. What he now discovered were what he thought of as indifferent narcissists repeating the views of the mainstream media on "the issues de jour" with an additional flourish along the lines of "their pussy cat predicted it all along". Even the smaller newspapers were hopeless. They relied on press releases, ignorant commentary and theft. They never reported the vitally significant leaks without WikiLeaks intervention. Counter-intuitively, only the major newspapers in the world, such as the *New York Times* or the *Guardian*, undertook any serious analysis but even they were self-censoring and their reportage dominated by the interests of powerful lobby groups. No one seemed truly interested in the vital material WikiLeaks offered or willing to do their own work. He wrote to his volunteers:

> What does it mean when only those facts about the world with economic powers behind them can be heard, when the truth lays [sic] naked before the world and no one will be the first to speak without a bribe?
>
> WikiLeaks' unreported material is only the most visible wave on an ocean of truth rotting in draws [sic] of the fourth estate, waiting for a lobby to subsidize its revelation into a profitable endeavour.

In Iraq, a junior American intelligence analyst, Private Bradley Manning – at least according to very convincing evidence yet to be tested in court – had been following WikiLeaks' activities with interest. On 25 November 2009 WikiLeaks released a document comprising 573,000 messages from September 11. As this material could only come from a National Security Agency leak, Manning was now convinced that WikiLeaks was genuine. Eventually, after sending WikiLeaks some cables concerning the American Ambassador in Iceland, he decided to download 93,000 logs from the Afghan War, 400,000 incident reports from the war in Iraq and 250,000 State Department cables, to which he and hundreds of thousands of American officials had access, and to send them to WikiLeaks. As a cover, he brought along Lady Gaga CDs and, while downloading these documents onto disc, pretended to be mouthing the words to the music. Some time after, he confessed to a convicted hacker, Adrian Lamo, what he had done. The most secure encryption and remailing systems were powerless against human, all-too-human frailty. Lamo in turn informed the FBI and American military authorities. Shortly after, Manning was arrested and taken to a military prison in West Virginia. Lamo also went with his evidence to a longstanding acquaintance, another convicted hacker, Kevin Poulsen, who worked at the magazine *Wired*. Poulsen published the log of some of the alleged conversation between Manning and Lamo.

(12.15:11 PM) bradass87: hypothetical question: if you had free reign [sic] over classified networks for long periods of time ... say 8-9 months ... and you saw incredible things, awful things ... things that belonged in the public domain, and not on some server stored in a dark room in Washington DC ... what would you do?

(12.26:09 PM) bradass87: lets just say "someone" I know intimately well, has been penetrating US classified

networks, mining data like the ones
described . . . and been transferring that
data from the classified networks over
the "air gap" onto a commercial network
computer . . . sorting the data, compress-
ing it, encrypting it, and uploading it
to a crazy white haired aussie who can't
seem to stay in one country very long.

One of the items sent to WikiLeaks was a video of a cold-blooded, American Apache helicopter attack on a group of Iraqis, in which up to fifteen men were gunned down. Assange made the decision to concentrate the resources and the energies of WikiLeaks on publishing it under the title: "Collateral Murder". In early April 2010, he flew to Washington to launch it, with his temporary chief-of-staff in Iceland (where the video had been edited), Rop Gonggrijp, the Dutch veteran of Berlin's Chaos Computer Club.

On 5 April, Assange addressed the National
Press Club. His frustration with the indifference of the world was, to put it mildly,
about to end.

*

For once, the cliché is true. What happened
over the next ten months is stranger than
fiction. With the release of the "Collateral Murder" footage, WikiLeaks became
instantly famous. Assange decided to
publish the new material he had received
from Manning anonymously in association
with some of the world's best newspapers or
magazines. Complex and heated negotiations
between WikiLeaks and the *Guardian*, the
New York Times and *Der Spiegel* were now
conducted. Even though these negotiations are one of the less interesting aspects
of this story, already three books from the
news outlets involved offering their own

perspectives have been published. Assange had long regarded the Western media as narcissistic. It is likely that his judgement was now confirmed.

In July the first of the Manning tranche, the "Afghan War Diary", was published. Assange held back only 15,000 of the 93,000 reports. Unforgivably, those released included the names of perhaps 300 Afghans who had assisted Western forces. A Taliban spokesperson, Zabiullah Mujahid, claimed that a nine-member commission had been created after the documents were released "to find out about people who were spying". Assange was unrepentant. In a speech in Sweden of 14 August, in talking about the practical impossibility of redacting names from the 93,000 reports, he distinguished between those who are "innocent" and those who are not. Regarding the latter he asked: "Are they entitled to retribution or not?" He did, however, learn from the experience. When the Iraq War logs were released in October most names had been redacted.

By now, fissures were emerging inside WikiLeaks. Relations between Assange and Domscheit-Berg became increasingly tense, especially after Assange warned him, in April 2010, regarding the exposure of sources: "If you fuck up, I'll hunt you down and kill you." Birgitta Jónsdóttir, the anarchist Icelandic parliamentarian, was concerned about what she saw as the cavalier way in which Assange had handled the moral issue of the Afghan War Diary. The young Icelandic anarchist historian, Herbert Snorrason, resented what he thought of as the increasingly dictatorial tendency inside the organisation. He claimed that Assange had warned: "I don't like your tone. If it continues you're out. I am the heart and soul of this organization, its founder, philosopher, spokesperson, original coder, organizer, financier, and all of the rest. If you have a problem . . . piss off."

On 21 August, Assange discovered that he was under investigation for sexual crimes after he slept with two Swedish supporters during a triumphal visit to Stockholm, one of whom, Anna Ardin, to complicate matters, had published advice on her blog concerning seven lawful kinds of revenge women might take after sexual mistreatment. Facing these charges, Assange expected total loyalty. Neither Domscheit-Berg nor Jónsdóttir were willing to give him what he wanted. Domscheit-Berg was suspended from WikiLeaks; Jónsdóttir quit. The man Domscheit-Berg called "the architect" followed. He and Domscheit-Berg took the WikiLeaks' submissions with them, at least temporarily, on the grounds that its sources needed far more scrupulous protection. Assange regards this as a pure "post facto fabrication". Yet there was more to the troubles at WikiLeaks than supposed concerns about Assange's laxity over security or his cavalier and dictatorial behaviour. In December, Rop Gonggrijp confessed to the Chaos Computer Club: "I guess I could make up all sorts of stories about how I disagreed with people or decisions, but the truth is that [during] the period that I helped out, the possible ramifications of WikiLeaks scared the bejezus out of me. Courage is contagious, my ass." Assange had taken on the power of the American state without flinching. His identification with Solzhenitsyn was no longer empty.

Assange decided to release the 250,000 US Department of State cables WikiLeaks still had in its possession on drip-feed so their content could be absorbed. On 28 November the first batch was published. The American vice president, Joe Biden, called

Assange a "high-tech terrorist". The rival vice-presidential candidate of 2008, Sarah Palin, thought he should be hunted down like Osama bin Laden, a suggestion that led Assange to quip to *Paris Match* that at least that option assured him of a further ten years of freedom. Visa, Mastercard and PayPal severed connections with WikiLeaks. A global guerrilla hacker army of WikiLeaks supporters, Anonymous, mounted an instant counter-attack.

Assange was by now facing two legal threats – extradition to Sweden to be interviewed about his relations with Anna Ardin and Sofia Wilén or extradition to the US where a secret grand jury had been established to look into whether he had committed crimes outlined in the 1917 *Espionage Act* or broken some other law. After a preliminary hearing in London on the Swedish extradition request, he was first imprisoned in

Wandsworth gaol and then placed under a form of house arrest.

In early April 2010 hardly anyone had heard of Julian Assange. By December he was one of the most famous people on Earth, with very powerful enemies and very passionate friends. A future extradition to the US was almost certain to ignite a vast Left versus Right global cultural war, a kind of 21st-century equivalent of the Dreyfus Affair. Ironically, if that broke out, his staunchest and most eloquent defenders were likely to be people Assange assured me he now genuinely admires, such as John Pilger or Tariq Ali or Michael Moore. These are the kind of thinkers whom Assange privately had once derided as followers of the "Progressive Commie Socialist" agenda. Domscheit-Berg tells us Assange considered Moore "an idiot". In an email Assange denied this with considerable eloquence: "I would never call someone as successful and influential as Moore an 'idiot'... His precise position is, I suspect, more a function of his market than his limitations. Similarly when people have called George W. Bush 'an idiot', I think they are wrong, and that they are wishfully blind to other forms of intelligence." In the coming cultural war, he would also be championed by millions of "average shy intellectuals" across the Western world who had watched on passively as the political and business elites and their spin-masters in the US and beyond plunged Iraq into bloody turmoil, brought chaos to the global financial markets and resisted action over the civilisational crisis of climate change.

Assange had long grasped the political significance of his compatriot, Rupert Murdoch. In "Conspiracy as Governance" he had called the disinformation the political and business elites fed the people to safeguard their power and their interests the "Fox News Effect". As the pressure on Assange mounted, Murdoch was clearly on his mind. In December, he spoke to Pilger in the *New Statesman* of an "insurance file" on Murdoch and News Corp his supporters would release if the future work of WikiLeaks was threatened by his arrest and to *Paris Match* about Murdoch's supposed "tax havens". If a culture war was engaged over Assange's extradition to the US it would involve, strangely enough, the clash of cultural armies mobilised by the creators of Fox News and WikiLeaks, the two most influential Australians of the era.

March 2011: Revised in light of a lengthy email exchange initiated by Julian Assange

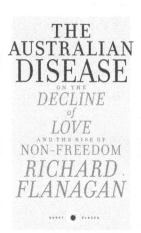

Richard Flanagan's perceptive, hilarious, searing exposé of the conformity that afflicts our public life.

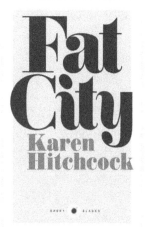

In a riveting blend of story and analysis, doctor and writer Karen Hitchcock explores chemistry, psychology and impulse to excess to explain the West's growing obesity epidemic.

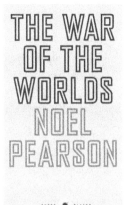

Noel Pearson considers
the most confronting issue
of Australian history:
the question of genocide,
in early Tasmania
and elsewhere.

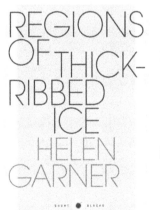

Helen Garner tells the tale
of a journey to Antarctica
aboard the *Professor
Molchanov*, spanning
icebergs, tourism, time,
photography and the many
forms of desolation.

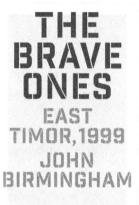

THE BRAVE ONES

EAST TIMOR, 1999

JOHN BIRMINGHAM

John Birmingham's unflinching account of the Indonesian Army's Battalion 745 as it withdrew from East Timor after the 1999 independence vote, leaving a trail of devastation in its wake.

BOOZE TERRITORY

ANNA KRIEN

Anna Krien takes a clear-eyed look at Indigenous binge-drinking, and never fails to see the human dimension of an intractable problem, shining a light on its deep causes.

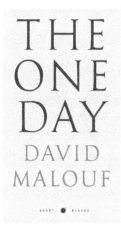

David Malouf traces the meaning of Anzac Day and shows how what was once history has now passed into legend, and how we have found in Anzac Day 'a truly national occasion.'

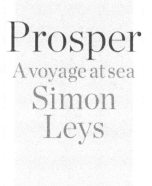

Simon Leys' exceptionally beautiful and elegiac essay about a summer spent on the crew of a tuna-fishing boat in Brittany.

SHORT ● BLACKS

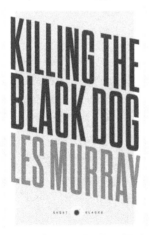

CYPHERPUNK
REVOLUTIONARY
ON
JULIAN
ASSANGE
ROBERT
MANNE

SHORT ● BLACKS

Robert Manne reveals the
making of Julian Assange
and shows how he became
one of the most influential
Australians of our time.

Les Murray's frank and
courageous account of his
struggle with depression.

WWW.SHORTBLACKS.COM

Robyn Davidson's fascinating and moving essay about nomads explores why, in times of environmental peril, the nomadic way with nature still offers valuable lessons.

Galarrwuy Yunupingu tells of his early life, his dealings with prime minsters, and how he learnt that nothing is ever what it seems.